COMPORTA
BLISS

To Pedro Espírito Santo and Vera Iachia

All photographs courtesy Carlos Souza & Charlene Shorto
Map illustration © Paola Le Faucheur

© 2018 Assouline Publishing
3 Park Avenue, 27th Floor
New York, NY 10016 USA
Tel.: 212-989-6769 Fax: 212-647-0005

www.assouline.com

Creative director: Camille Dubois
Art directors: Jihyun Kim & Paola Naugès
Editorial director: Esther Kremer
Editor: Lindsey Tulloch
Printed in China.
ISBN: 9781614286264
10 9 8 7 6 5 4 3 2

TEXT BY CARLOS SOUZA

PHOTOGRAPHY BY CARLOS SOUZA
& CHARLENE SHORTO

COMPORTA
BLISS

ASSOULINE

COMPORTA

Plage de Comporta

Praia de Peixe

Carvalhal

66 Comporta is untouched nature, where you can smell all Mother Earth's aromas, hear all sounds, and taste all flavors from the living ground. **99**

—Marina Espírito Santo Saldanha

I was born in Brazil, a fourth-generation Portuguese descendant. During my first trip to Portugal in the late 1970s, my dear friend Pedro Espírito Santo took me to Comporta. The Espírito Santos had a vast expanse of land with rice fields and very few houses. The land was quite remote and simple in structure, yet so rich in a sensorial way. Back then, access to Comporta's beautiful beaches was gained via the Tróia peninsula, and visitors had to use the ferry crossing to make the journey.

Cities I visit have always been imprinted in my memory thanks to my sensitive nose. With each fresh destination, my first encounter with the perfumes of local cuisine, vegetation, and flora is the prelude to a new love affair. The curry of Delhi, the *dendê* or palm oil of Salvador, the rosemary of Sardinia, the frangipani flowers of Bali, and the desert aroma of Marrakech are just a few examples. As with these and the many other places on this planet that I love, my olfactory sense played a big role during my first visit to

Comporta. My first impression was the fragrance of this village, a huge plantation of verdant pines giving off a pungent perfume. These expanses of trees are composed of two species and shapes: the *pinheiro manso,* or stone pine, and *pinheiro bravo,* or maritime or cluster pine. The Espírito Santo family planted both varieties when they bought the property.

Comporta is a twenty-five-mile span of beach that stretches from Tróia to Melides, boasting white sands and clear green waters—almost always cold currents of the north Atlantic Ocean—married to blue skies and fresh Atlantic air. Nature is quite wild in the Alentejo region, which pairs wonderfully with the sweet, simpatico mood of the locals. Tradition and folklore, like the Portuguese soul, are colorful. It's the balance of all these elements that creates the unique experience and environment that is Comporta. The entire region is ruled by the rice fields, which are the ideal ecosystem. The large quantities of water needed to grow the rice lead to lots of mosquitoes, which in turn attract frogs to the rice paddies, which in turn attract the beautiful storks that migrate from Africa in the summer to lay their eggs in nests built on chimneys or lampposts in town. The baby storks learn how to fly in the rice fields in midsummer, soaring back to Africa when winter approaches. It is all a delicate equilibrium.

Opposite, clockwise from top left: Birds are an important part of the ecosystem in Comporta; a stretch of soft white sand leading to the beautiful coast; a mixture of azulejo tiles from the seventeenth, eighteenth, and nineteenth centuries; a window painted with the region's signature cobalt blue tone.
Previous pages: Rice fields make up a large part of Comporta's landscape.
Following pages: Homes in Comporta respect and blend easily with the natural surroundings.

Manuel Espírito Santo, one of the former owners of the Herdade da Comporta estate, and his family, photographed in Lisbon.

Food is very important in Portuguese tradition, and in this region, fish is king. The cold north-Atlantic waters are responsible for the freshest fish and crustaceans, which acquire a special flavor after undergoing the many tricks of Portuguese seasoning, *o bom tempero português!* My preferred dish in Comporta, which was also my first meal there, is the *amêijoas à bulhão pato,* which is all about fresh clams cooked with garlic cloves and cilantro—simple and delicious. Throughout the region, flavors abound for the expert palate. Young Portuguese wine is another of my favorites. Served by the glass from pressure machines at local bars, with only six percent alcohol, it is a fresh and restoring cure and palate cleanser.

After a long hiatus of about ten years, I returned to Portugal and was once again completely captivated by its unaltered simplicity. Unlike Europe's many other summer paradises, Comporta has maintained its authenticity and has not been polluted by big corporations selling their coffees, burgers, and high-end fashions. Local markets distribute fruits and vegetables from the region's farmers, as well as their wines from the great Alentejo region. Weekend markets and fairs still showcase all the local artisanal wares, simple and sincere in their functions. In this world of global corporations, all this is quite a blessing.

Nowadays, the magical city of Lisbon attracts travelers from all over the world with its charm—not to mention its convenient prices. Walking the city's streets, one now hears French being spoken along with Portuguese. Italians are retiring to the region's towns and fields, pulled by the magnetism of the simple, sweet Portuguese soul.

Comporta itself hosts an incredible array of houses. While most are vacation homes, there is a growing colony of year-round foreigners that includes a colorful French influence, its international, sophisticated taste marrying perfectly with the local simplicity. The colors of Comporta are white and blue, the latter an Yves Klein shade that matches the skies, and the light along the Atlantic shores is inimitable, making it easy to wake up early to witness the enchantment of dawn.

Recently, hotels such as Sublime are being built in the region, and summer rental homes are a popular option. It's wise to book a summer home just as the year begins. In early August, families that have been coming to Comporta for years migrate to their inland country homes, returning once the summer crowd is gone near the end of the month.

Unlike so many summer places I visit that have, with time, lost their luster and attraction for me, my desire to visit Comporta holds strong. With its original soul, folklore, genuineness, outstanding cuisine, and loving openness of its people, who could ask for more?

Bem-vindo a Comporta!

CARLOS SOUZA

Above: An idyllic Comporta beach scene.
Opposite: Storks migrate from Africa to lay their eggs in Comporta and teach their babies to fly in the rice fields.
Following pages: Blue amphoras at Vera Iachia's home represent the essence of Comporta.

66 The first time I visited Comporta thirty years ago, I stayed at Pedro Espírito Santo's home during the early stages of its design. Pedro is a magical interior decorator who loves to change his decor all the time and with the seasons, an exercise that is now also a favorite hobby of mine on relaxed weekends. As he explained to me, the base for his simple, curious, and colorful mix is the result of visiting the homes of humble peasants in the Nova Friburgo area of Brazil, two hours away from Rio de Janeiro where we own neighboring country homes in the mountains. Pedro is passionate about visiting Portuguese country fairs on weekends to hunt for marvelous pieces that add character to his shabby-chic approach and match his overall vision for his home. 99

" This has been the Espírito Santo family's estate since they first bought land in Comporta. Its traditional Portuguese rooms are marked by a flair for Chinese porcelain. The Espírito Santos told me that their journey to spend long periods of the summer at this country home used to take days, since they would travel by oxcart with all their staff and luggage and the area had no roads. "

"The property also includes a beautiful church filled with classic Portuguese furniture and stunning azulejos, or glazed ceramic tilework pieces, where many happy family ceremonies have taken place over the years."

66 The color palette in François Simon's home is very calm, warm, and soothing on the eyes, and it makes a great contrast to the rice fields and fabulous views the house offers, being on top of the vast terrain filled with verdant rice in the summer months. The use of local straw and wicker and contemporary shapes gives a modern feel to this chic and elegant home. 99

"My first stay at Sublime, a wonderful hotel situated in the middle of a cork forest, was some seven or eight years ago, when there were only twelve bungalows and the main house. Since then, thirty-five more bungalows have been added, their design a seamless balance between contemporary and rustic. The use of local wood and a color palette with marine undertones works perfectly when surrounded by nature. The social area and restaurants are luminous, and the hotel also boasts a great spa. This is considered a new destination for weddings and other events in the Muda area."

66 Someone once said that Comporta is praise of slowness. It's a perfect definition. We come here for the light, the quiet, the purity, the straw cabanas under the clear sky, the kindness of the locals. We come here for nothing. The village is simple. It's not an idyllic scene for a postcard, but it's a true village. The forest planted in the sand is immense and savage. We can feel alone in the world here. 99

Daniel Suduca and Thierry Mérillou

Above: A pop-up shop in the Casa da Cultura da Comporta museum.
Opposite, clockwise from top left: The Stork Club, Jaques Grange and Pierre Passebon's home decor shop in Carvalhal; pop-up shops in the Casa da Cultura; Santa Maria Velharias, José Antonio Brito Canudo's antique shop in Carvalhal.

66

66 Ana Cristina Nasi's home was constructed by her dear sister Pequenina Rodrigues, a longtime friend of mine who has sadly passed away. Ana Cristina's joy for living can be felt in the way she entertains her always-funny guests with the help of her gourmand husband, Carlo Nasi, who makes an exquisite spaghetti *alla bottarga.* 99

" Ana Cristina and Carlo's home decor is respectful of the region's color palette, and they have an enchanting tree house that I was lucky enough to sleep in, waking up to the chirping of a zillion birds having a feast in the rice fields. "

Vem! a casita é modesta,
mas quando surge um amigo,
parece um castelo em festa.

Bulhão Pato

66 We just completed the construction of two Timor houses, a design from the nineteenth century. Raised off the sand, they aim to provide a feeling of rebirth every evening under the dome of the sky and every morning with a thousand birds passing by. **99**

Louis Albert and Françoise de Broglie

66 **Comporta is the perfume of freedom and essential emotions, the perfume of life and gifts of nature, the perfume of promises.** 99

Louis Albert and Françoise de Broglie

66 For me, Caetana Beirão da Veiga's home uses one of the best color palettes referring back to the area. The blues and greens play a symphony of colors in contrast to the rice fields, and the home has a feeling of summer, peace, and gaiety all at the same time. The design is also true to the region in terms of construction, respecting the structures left by homes of times past. 99

"Straw from the rice fields is bound together to make the roofs of many buildings in Comporta—just another way the homes here blur the line between interior and natural exterior."

Above: Antonio Pinela, thatched construction specialist, with his *cabanas de colmo* miniatures.
Opposite, clockwise from top left: Daniela de Camaret, Luis Felipe Diniz, and Charlene Shorto; a bread oven at Vera Iachia's home; Ana Cristina Nasi, Carlos Souza, and Vera Iachia; Barracuda vintage interiors shop owner Alexandre Neimann.

"It's so rare in Europe to arrive, after only a short flight, in undisturbed nature with storks nesting everywhere and be able to sleep to the sound of the ocean. Comporta is a place out of a poem by Rilke. In one word, supercalifragilisticexpialidocious, as Mary Poppins said!"

Suzanne Syz

66 **The Hotel dos Mosquitos is based entirely on the Mongolian** *ger*, **or yurt. These round structures made with bamboo and canvas are the ideal start to a fabulous vacation, transporting guests completely with their dreamy summer setting, simple and surrounded by Comporta's natural rice fields. Blue stripes and green tones characterize this boutique hotel, a remote, isolated seaside dream perfect for a honeymoon.** 99

66 **The immense, protected, natural beach is a miracle. But first-time visitors need friends to guide them, or they might have a hard time understanding the area beyond the beach.** 99

Jacques Grange and Pierre Passebon

66 The perfect day in Comporta is not having a plan and deciding in the moment. 99

Jacques Grange and Pierre Passebon

66 Lara and Carloto Beirão da Veiga and their family love entertaining. Their house is filled with young people, so they emphasize teaching the next generation how to entertain in the traditional Portuguese way. 99

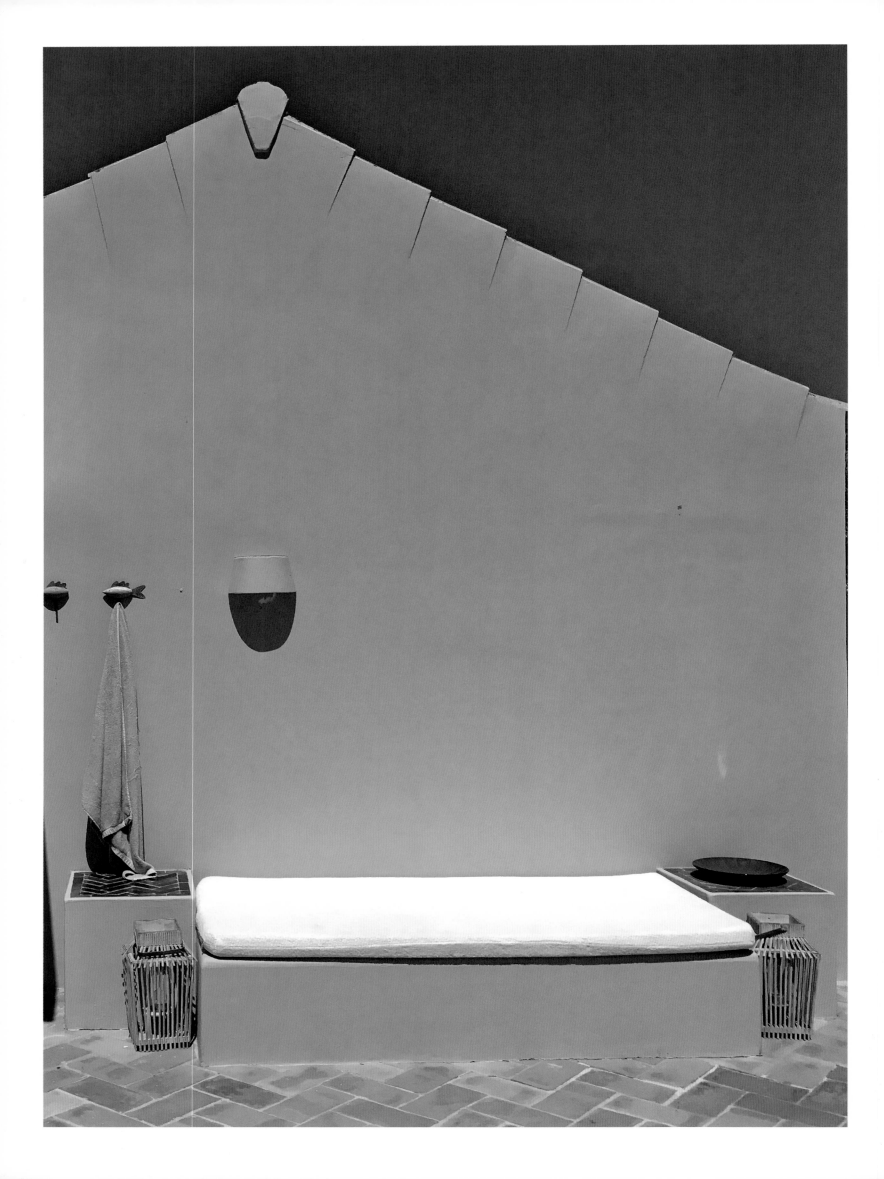

66 Marina Espírito Santo Saldanha's house is joyful, colorful, and very true to Comporta's typical aesthetic. She loves visiting fairs, and her home's souvenirs reflect her many travel memories. The way she mixes and matches to juxtapose the pieces is curious, smart, and very charming indeed. Marina also has a store in Carvalhal where, every summer, a new line of pieces bursting with color reproduces the vision of her travels. 99

"Comporta's seafood is unparalleled, and my favorite are the clams. Other cuisine highlights include the many varieties of cheese, Pêra-Manca wine, and the *bola de Berlim,* or Berliner donut."

66 A longtime friend of mine and a muse to so many fashion worlds, Farida Khelfa has a home that makes visitors feel relaxed and complete. The decor is minimalist, white rooms touched with strokes of color found in the objects and furniture. 99

66 Farida's gardens are wonderful, and her home's structure is very grounded in the aesthetics of the Portuguese coast, complete with Comporta blue. And of course, her over-the-top humor and presence fill every room. 99

Above: Joana Leitão Zanotta's piadina truck, a 2017 summer success.
Opposite, clockwise from top left: Senhor Luis poses with a scarecrow as he cares for his organic vegetable garden;
Rogério at Pica Peixe specializes in samosas; a local citizen; police on horseback in Carvalhal.

66 Recently, I visited Comporta with friends and family for a fifteen-day vacation, and we stayed at Marta Mosqueira do Amaral's magical home. Colorful, playful, and filled with character, it is one of the best examples of shabby-chic I know of and among the most glorious vacation destinations I have ever experienced. 99

66 Every morning while at Marta's, waking up and eating breakfast together, we felt so joyous. We genuinely enjoyed photographing this beautiful and whimsical space. 99

"The sounds are mainly from the ocean, but you can also hear the toads and frogs in the rice fields and the cooing of the turtledoves, who wake me up each morning as they perch on my bedroom fireplace."

Patrick Perrin

“Near my house is Denize, the canteen I adore. It's open all year round, and I have sat inside with my family during February vacation, when we were the only guests, looking out at the raging sea and the pouring rain, eating delicious local fish and thinking of Portuguese history, the parting ships and fado singers. But I also like to cook big meals made with local products at my house and invite my neighbors.”

Renate Graff

Carlos at the Sado Estuary Natural Reserve, where the local fishermen keep their boats and hold cuttlefish auctions.

66 This house, situated in the Vale Perdido, is the home of dear Luiz Saldanha. Its decor is an ethnic mix of curious lost-and-found pieces procured throughout his many years of travels. One can spend hours here exploring, lost in seclusion in the valley near the rice fields. Luiz is a man of many hats and ideas and a wonderful storyteller, and culture and education abound in his home. In the words of Luiz himself, 'Comporta is a love affair.' 99

"Comporta is unspoiled nature, sun, peace. Magnificent landscapes, miles and miles of empty white sandy beaches, pine trees. The scent of lavender in the dunes mingled with all the wildflowers. The birds on the rice fields."

Françoise Dumas

"When I moved into my home in Carvalhal, my friend Karl Lagerfeld offered me a selection of the works of Eça de Queiros, one of the greatest Portuguese novelists, and I was totally seduced by his book *Os Maias*."

Françoise Dumas

"Comporta is lavender and sea breeze."

Benedita Nunes de Matos

" Benedita's home has a clean-slate feeling, contemporary and sleek. Nature surrounds the property, and ample spaces with cement hues are the norm. The Olympic-size swimming pool is the young ones' favorite spot from dawn to dusk on summer days. Benedita is a gourmet, and the soul of the home lies in her colorful culinary skills. She cooks delicious, traditional Portuguese cuisine, a contrast to her modern home. The aromas of her plates perfume the house, and she produces fine wines to pair with them— a truly winning combination. "

Following pages: Carvalhal Beach.

"Florence Grinda is my longtime friend from Paris, and it was a great surprise to learn she bought a home in Comporta. I had to visit at just the right time to capture her lovely gardens—a nod of recognition to Louis Benech, who created a fabulous combination of verdant plants and flowers local to the region (and also worked on Paris's Jardin des Tuileries). Florence's home is situated atop the rice fields, offering an unparalleled view. Through her impeccable taste in decoration, one can feel how much she enjoyed ornamenting her home with vibrant, well-chosen pieces, perfectly placed to give a playful, happy feeling."

Above: Fishing boat on Comporta Beach.
Opposite, clockwise from top left: Dried and salted cod; Pôr do Sol restaurant in Carvalhal; earthenware fish by artist Rafael Bordallo Pinheiro in Albert and Françoise de Broglie's kitchen; Rei do Choco in Carrasqueira specializes in cuttlefish.

"Philippe Starck's Comporta home is raised on stilts with a grand staircase, a veritable tree house perched among the eucalyptus and umbrella pines."

Above: Locally made wares at Vera Iachia's shop in Carvalhal.
Opposite, clockwise from top left: Glass and woven crafts in Vera Iachia's shop; Barracuda, an interior design store
with vintage pieces that opened in spring 2018 in Carvalhal; Senhor Carlos's vintage shop in Carvalhal.

"When Charlene and I began collecting photos for this book, we were invited to stay with Vera Iachia on her beautiful property. We spent wonderful days going in and out, always so glad to return to this enchanted place she created over her many long years in Comporta. The cobalt-blue amphoras in her garden epitomize Vera's vision of paradise. The property's many homes are luxurious yet simple, and the gardens are a shining example of the incredible ecosystem that reigns here. Vera was a perfectionist with impeccable taste, a warm, receiving host, and a dedicated ambassador of Comporta. Her cuisine was delicious and exquisitely presented. Her staff adored her as a mentor, not a manager. She had an interior decor boutique in Carvalhal where I bought countless pieces that are scattered among my homes. Charlene and I miss Vera greatly."

Above: The entrance to Vera Iachia's property.
Opposite: Vera's boats in the rice lagoon.

DIRECTORY

RESTAURANTS

CAVALARIÇA
Dinner only in the old stables. Great food and design. Tell the owners, CJ and Roberta Morell, that I sent you.
Rua do Secador 9, 7580
+351 930 451 879
cavalaricacomporta.com

COLMO BAR
A smoothie and juice bar.
Largo de São João
+93 42 345 5578

COMPORTA CAFÉ
A nice place for drinks.
Praia da Comporta, 7680-612
+351 265 497 652
comportacafe.com.pt

EUCALYPTUS
This café, across the street from Gomes, has pastries, orange juice, and other breakfast items, and makes great sandwiches for the beach.
Rua do Comércio 1, 7580-742
+351 966 641 845

GLORIA
Known for their grilled chicken.
Brejos da Carregueira de Baixo
+351 265 497 160

GOMES SUPERMERCADOS
This grocery store has everything, including items for beach picnics and a good selection of wine and liquor. The owner speaks English.
Rua do Comércio 4, 7580-642
+351 265 497 031

ILHA DO ARROZ
Great atmosphere, great food, and one of the most beautiful esplanades on the Costa Azul.
7570-789 Carvalhal
+351 265 490 510

O GERVÁSIO
Go where the locals go for excellent pasta or rice with fish.
Brejos da Carregueira de Baixo
+351 265 497 111

PIADINAS ZANOTTA
Street food served from Joana Leitão Zanotta's truck in Comporta village.
+351 910 982 001

PICA PEIXE
Notable dishes include crab curry, samosas, and roast beef sandwiches.
Avenida 18 de Dezembro 21A
Carvalhal
+351 265 490 277

PÔR DO SOL
One of our favorite beach spots. The freshest fish and traditional Portuguese seaside cuisine.
Carvalhal Beach 7570-782
+351 265 497 225
pordosol-restaurante.com

RESTAURANTE DONA BIA
A sandwich place on the side of the road in Torre with very good, basic food.
N261, Torre, 7580-681
+351 265 497 557

RESTAURANTE MUSEU DO ARROZ
This restaurant serves fresh seafood and is very nice for a fun dinner. Tell the owner, Isabelinha Carvalho, that I sent you.
Estrada Nacional 261 Km 0, 7580-612
+351 265 497 555

RESTAURANTE O DINIS
On Praia do Carvalhal. Less glam than Sal, but they serve good, solid fish.
Quinta da Fontanheira, Lote 6
Lajeosa Oliveira do Hospital, Carvalhal
+351 967 977 193

RESTAURANTE O ROLA
Try the fried calamari.
Rua da Fonte
+351 265 497 003

RESTAURANTE O TOBIAS
Seafood and a beer garden.
7570-782 Grândola
+351 265 490 236

RESTAURANTE SABOR DO MAR
A good pick for sea bream and sea bass.
Rua do Comercio 17
+351 265 497 185

RESTAURANTE SAL
The best restaurant and bar on Pego Beach. Great fish. Make a reservation here for lunch or an early dinner during the sunset. For a proper beach day, park in the paying lot at Praia do Pego and get chairs on the beach at the restaurant.
Praia do Pego, Carvalhal, 7570-783
+351 265 490 129
restaurantesal.pt

SHOPPING

A LOJA DO MUSEU DO ARROZ
A treasure trove of everything from crockery to caftans, fabrics, and woven straw hats.
Largo de São João 8 7580-612
+351 927 153 677

ANTIQUÁRIO JOSÉ ANTONIO BRITO CANUDO
Souvenirs, furniture, crockery, and decorations.
Avenida 18 de Dezembro, 16
Carvalhal
+351 916 296 639

BABOUCHETTE
Barberine Agier's store with accessories and items for a Comporta lifestyle.
Becos da Comporta 2
+351 265 497 645

BARRACUDA
A brand-new home decor shop.
Avenida 18 de Dezembro 19
7570-779 Carvalhal
barracuda-comporta.com

CORAL
Nature-inspired home goods.
Rua do Secador, 7580-624
+351 919 858 721

CÔTÉ-SUD
Colorful sandals, embroidered cover-ups, and furniture accessories.
Largo de São João 3 7580-624
+351 265 497 317

LAVANDA
Catherine Austad's shop next to the Novo Banco, with great coffee and natural juices, clothes, and home goods. She also has a shop in Lisbon.
Largo de São João 3, 7580-624
+351 265 098 364

LOJA DE CÁ
Marina Espírito Santo Saldanha's shop of baskets and home goods.
Avenida 18 de Dezembro 42
+351 265 490 438

MANUMAYA
Beautiful and colorful products from Guatemala, including bedcovers, clothing, and bags.
+351 914 109 360
manumaya.com

RICE
Marta Mantero's furniture accessories supply shop.
Estrada Nacional 253 Km 1 7580-612
+ 351 969 571 739
martamantero.com

STORK CLUB
Jacques Grange and Pierre Passebon's home decor shop in Carvalhal.
+351 265 497 766

TM COLLECTION
Fashion and summer beach apparel.
Largo São João, 3 -1° 7850-624
+ 351 265 497 360
tmcollection.com

VINTAGE-DEPARTMENT
Decorators' merchants.
Rua do Secador, 7580-648
+351 911 778 837
vintage-department.com

BEACHES

Some of the beaches in Algarve, such as **Praia dos Três Irmãos** or **Praia do Camilo**, are tiny coves curtained by low cliffs. Others, like **Praia de São Rafael** and **Praia do Carvalho**, are embellished with caves and sea-carved archways where you can find shelter from the heat of the day.

Then there are the lively sand strips where people come to be in a crowd, including **Praia de Monte Gordo** and **Praia de Tavira**. Explore Tavira Town and the Lagos fish market.

Make sure to visit **Praia do Pego** and have lunch at Sal, or try **Praia da Comporta**.

If you take a day trip to **Sol Tróia**, about 25 minutes away, you can visit **Praia Atlantica** there, which is also amazing.

The nicest beach is **Vigia**, south of Aberta Nova. It's completely deserted and not signposted. Coming south on the N261 to Melides, the town is on the left. Turn right at the sign for the *cemiterio* (graveyard), pass the graveyard on the right with the lagoon on your left, and follow the dirt track straight all the way to the end. There's a small parking lot there for just a few cars. From here, walk to the beach—but make sure to bring your own picnic since there are no restaurants nearby.

OTHER ATTRACTIONS

Reserve a horseback ride on the beach (well in advance, as it fills up quickly) with my friend Ze Ribeira at **Cavalos na Areia**. Coming north from Comporta, it's just after the village of Torre on the left. It's an unforgettable experience; tell him I sent you. They do two rides per morning.
Estrada Nacional N261
Km 6, Torre 7580-681
+351 919 002 545
cavalosnaareia.com

About an hour south of Comporta, stop in **Sines** and visit the **Castelo de Sines**. Have lunch at one of the sweet little *tascas*, local shacks that look very provincial but often have unbelievable food.
Rua do Muro da Praia, 7520-151 Sines
+351 269 630 600

PORTO COVO

Praia dos Aivados is the famous beach here, just a twelve-minute drive from the town, and it's not to be missed. You should also drive to **Praia do Malhão**, about 25 minutes away, since it's one of the best beaches in all of Portugal— super secluded and absolutely massive. No beach bar or bathrooms, so plan meals ahead or bring food.

If you're driving farther south to Odeceixe (doable in a day as it's about an hour away), visit **Praia da Amália**: It's one of the most impressive beaches I've ever been to.

ALENTEJO

Barrocal is a great base to explore from. Return to Lisbon via Évora and spend a day here. There's a nice spa and a pool where you can spend the hottest hours of the day; the rooms are air-conditioned. The food in Barrocal is superb. I recommend **Restaurante Sabores de Monsaraz**, which has a lovely view and a terrace and serves good Alentejano dishes. Note that they're closed on Mondays.
Rua de São Bento 2, 7200-175
+351 969 217 800
saboresdemonsaraz.com

If you ride horses, there's an *equitador*, Filipe, who can take you for a two-hour trip from Barrocal up to **Monsaraz** and through the town. It was amazing when I went—I recommend early morning or evening. If you don't ride, he can bring you around the town by carriage.

On the way to Évora, visit the **Adega Herdade do Esporão** winery outside Reguengos.
Apartado 31 999 Distrito de Évora
Alentejo, 7200
Reguengos de Monsaraz
+351 266 509 280
esporao.com

In **Évora**, park near the *pousada* (inn) and walk around. See the **Capela dos Ossos** and **Praça do Giraldo**; visit the roof of the **Cathedral of Évora** for amazing views; and stop at the small **Museu de Évora**. Finish with the **Convento dos Lóios**. Have a drink at the *quiosque* (newsstand) or on the patio of the **Palace of the Dukes of Cadaval** next door.

CAPELA DOS OSSOS
Praça 1º de Maio 4, 7000-650

CATHEDRAL OF ÉVORA
Largo do Marquês
  de Marialva 809, 7000
+351 266 759 330

MUSEU DE ÉVORA
Largo do Conde de Vila Flor, 7000-804
+351 266 730 480
museudevora.pt

CONVENTO DOS LÓIOS
Rua Dr. Santos Carneiro 7,
Santa Maria da Feira
+351 256 331 070

For dining in Évora, I recommend the classic **Restaurante Fialho**— but reserve a terrace in the bar, which is more casual. Around the corner is the best restaurant in town: **Tasquinha do Oliveira**. The owner was the maître d' at Fialho. It's amazing but very heavy, so I would go for dinner instead of lunch.

RESTAURANTE FIALHO
Tv. das Mascarenhas 16, 7000-557
+351 266 703 079
restaurantefialho.pt

TASQUINHA DO OLIVEIRA
Rua Cândido dos Reis 45, 7000
+351 266 744 841

If you're driving on to **Estremoz**, the **Saturday Market** is great. Drive back to Barrocal via Vila Viçosa and Alandroal, through the beautiful countryside.

ACKNOWLEDGMENTS

Carlos and Charlene would like to thank all
their friends who hosted them in Comporta and
introduced them to the regional lifestyle gently and
gradually, and they hope everyone who travels there
has the fortune to experience the same guidance.
Thank you to Martine and Prosper Assouline and
their team for all their help in bringing Comporta
to life within these pages.

The publisher would like to thank Phyllis Goodale
for her invaluable work on this book.

ABOUT THE AUTHORS

Carlos Souza is the worldwide brand ambassador for Valentino and has over forty years of experience in fashion. His career as a photographer was initiated by Andy Warhol, for whom he used to work photographing fashion shows for *Interview*. Known as an art world and fashion fixture, Souza is also an editor at large for *Architectural Digest* and contributing editor for *Interview*. Recently, his refined taste and passion for fashion inspired him to launch his own line of jewelry, Most Wanted Design. His book *#Carlos's Places* was published by Assouline in 2014.

Charlene Shorto was born in Recife, Brazil, and educated in Switzerland and Great Britain. She married Carlos Souza and had two sons, Sean and Anthony. The family moved to Rome, where Charlene worked in fashion with Valentino Garavani and became the director of Oliver by Valentino, traveling the globe to all press and fashion show events. Nowadays, Charlene lives in Lisbon, a city she has loved since childhood and where she has many dear friends. She has spent time in Comporta since her teen years, and this book demonstrates her passion for photography and her special eye for nature and decor.

Charlene and Carlos photographed at Pedro Espírito Santo's home.